Summer 81

I wish for you
prosperity + adventure
and far from all
the seasons of your
life

Jim Rohn

ACKNOWLEDGEMENTS

To My Mother and Father . . . who taught me that life and business is like the changing seasons.

To Dan McBride . . . whose constant loyalty and unshakeable persistence will never be forgotten.

To Ron Reynolds . . . who finds unique ways for more people to hear and share our ideas.

To All Those Who Contributed . . . from my early years until now. The audience which you've provided to me, both public and private, large and small—in conversation or in seminar, forces me to find new ways to share my deepest thoughts. Each of you will know how you've touched me.

. . . and to Nora Weinberger, whose creativity in art speaks for itself from the pages of this book.

THE
SEASONS
OF
LIFE

by
E. James Rohn

Discovery Publications
2091 Business Center Drive
Irvine, CA 92715
(714) 851-0863

Copyright© 1981 By Jim Rohn Productions

Published By Discovery Publications
Irvine, California

First Printing, April 1981

Library of Congress Card Catalog No: 81-66145
ISBN No.: 0-939490-00-5
Designed by Ronald L. Reynolds
Manufactured in the United States of America

CONTENTS

Nora Weinberger
Illustrator

NORA'S ARK
ARTWORK & DESIGN

P.O. Box 1225
Costa Mesa, CA 92626
(714) 966-1988

FORWORD

John Kennedy once remarked that Winston Churchill "mobilized the English language and sent it into battle." Past generations have heard the stirring words of Cicero, Daniel Webster, Disraeli, Churchill and Kennedy . . . men touched by their creator with the gift of changing the course of human history and the quality of the individual life through their well-spoken words.

Jim Rohn, a man of our own generation, has been given such a gift. His inspiring seminars and appearances before groups across America and around the world has changed the lives of tens of thousands. He has the unique capacity for finding the miraculous hidden among the common, and for expressing it with word pictures that uniquely affect all who listen.

"The Seasons Of Life" is but a momentary glimpse at the depth of the character of Jim Rohn. His ability for reawakening the sleeping spirit residing within us all is most welcome in a time of change and challenge. While this book is the first by Mr. Rohn, it surely will not be his last. My association with him in preparing this book has made me aware that the world needs to know more of this man. His ideas on goals, personal development, leadership skills, and the value of effective communications are needed in all areas of education, of government, and in business . . . and his contribution to improving the quality of family life is immeasureable.

This book may well be destined to become a masterpiece in literary creativity.

Ronald L. Reynolds

THE
SEASONS
OF
LIFE

I. THE CYCLES AND SEASONS OF LIFE

For six thousand years of recorded history, humans have entered this world, received parental instruction, classroom instruction, and gathered the experience of life; many have set for themselves ambitious goals, and dreamed lofty dreams, but upon the day that they draw their last breath, have left little behind as evidence of their existence other than a birth certificate, gravemarker, and one-half million dollars in consumed goods and services between their humble beginnings and uneventful end.

Books have been authored on the subject of human achievement, seminars are conducted on how to find success, and those who have met with and embraced success willingly share their ideas and insights with all those who will listen.

For some, worldly riches are gained at the price of lost friends and broken families. For others, fortune remains forever elusive, while families remain precariously intact. For most, we remain forever in one of two categories—either poor, seeking to become wealthy or wealthy, seeking always to rediscover the happiness we had while we were poor.

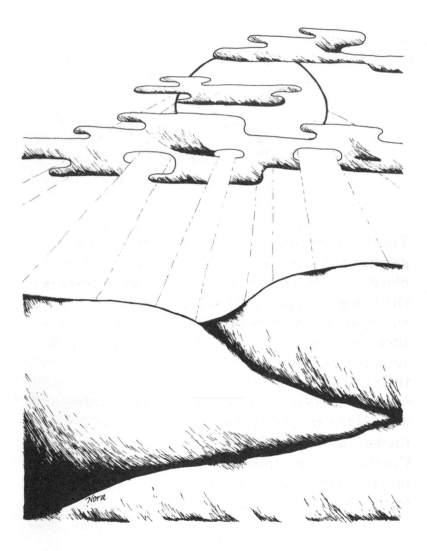

This book, a condensation of ideas and observations gained over a period of four decades will attempt to place life, its events, purpose, opportunities and challenges into perspective. It is not intended to be an instructional treatise on either how to achieve success or how to avoid failure. If life were to hold such precise answers to age-old questions, surely their discovery would now be history and each of us would now be living to enjoy our success. In truth, what is the formula for success for one will lead to the self-destruction of another. As certainly as our Creator made us individually unique, so did He also preserve for each of us individually unique answers to the challenge of life.

It is the purpose of this book, therefore, to awaken within each of us, the storehouse of inspiration and answers that lies sleeping where they have been since being placed there at birth—within the hearts and minds of each of us.

Let us now seek to discover our own individual answers to our own individual challenges by exploring the cycles and *seasons of life.*

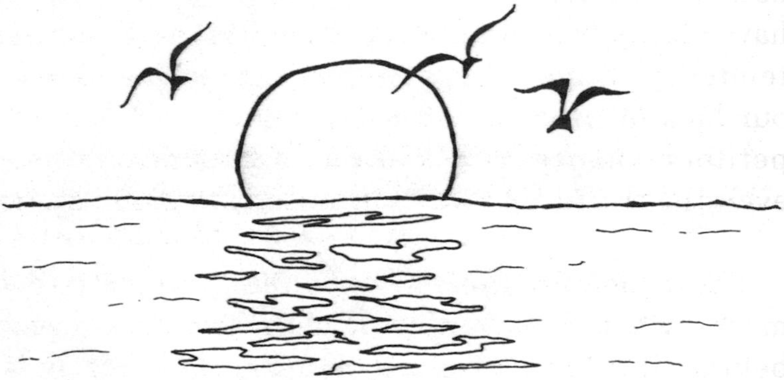

II. THE EFFECT OF ENVIRONMENT ON CIRCUMSTANCE

All of us, whether rich or poor, young or old, educated or not so educated, are the sum total of all of those people and events that have touched us since first entering this world. Every thought we've entertained has had its effect upon what we now are. Every movie we've watched had its effect. Every book or magazine we've read had its effect. Every TV show has had its effect. Every disappointment, triumph, doubt, dream, and love for someone each had *their* effect. What we *are* and what we *have,* we have slowly brought upon *ourselves.* It is the human tendency to blame someone or something else for our lack of progress—we blame government, competitors, managers, inflation, pay schedules and even the traffic and weather for our circumstances.

Those people and events which have left their mark—whether favorable or unfavorable—are now behind us. What happened even as recently as yesterday is no longer of any consequence, unless we choose to allow it to be. What is of great importance is *who* and *what* it is that leaves its mark *today,* and each day thereafter. What we *have been* is an established and unchangeable fact. What we can *yet become* is an unlimited, boundless *opportunity.* Therefore, do not allow your awareness of past difficulty or failures to adversely affect your current and future possibilities. The greatest value of the past is how wisely we invest it in the future. Let the *past* be a *servant* for making the *future* both more enjoyable and profitable.

For those who seriously accept that they deserve and will one day achieve financial independence, let each break off the "rear-view mirror" of their lives and concentrate upon what lies ahead. Let them begin their quest for achievement by taking a close inventory of those people and circumstances which today touch their lives, for it is *their* effect which will determine what lies ahead—what the size of the *next* crop will be come *next* fall.

We sometimes can accumulate a mixture of the people and environments of life which, if not altered in some way, will assure that our future will be just about like our past. Positive human progress has its price, for surely, each gain *automatically* produces a loss or a sacrifice. Each of us is affected in a negative way by *something* each day. One of the great challenges of life is to have both the wisdom to recognize those sources of negativity, and the courage to cast them aside, if necessary. None of us would voluntarily drink a glass of deadly poison if we knew what it was, and yet each of us has friends, or relatives, or business associates whose affect on us is just as deadly as the glass of poison. The difference is that

one form of poison kills instantly — once consumed, the body recoils, weakens, and then all bodily functions cease. Other "poisons" kill hope, ambition, enthusiasm, and the thirst for achievement. The methods are different, but the ultimate result is the same. There is little difference between one who has given up his life and one who has given up his hope.

There are those who will laugh at those who read useful books, and yet there is little difference between those who *cannot* read and those who *will not* read—the result of both is ignorance.

There are those who will discourage those in search of a better occupation, and yet it is essential that each of us find what we were "meant to do" if true happiness is to be found.

There are those who will frown upon those who set ambitious goals, and yet without goals there can be no achievement, and without achievement life will be as it has been.

There are those who will gossip about those who are doing well, and yet there can be no cause for rejoicing among those who are doing poorly.

There are those who will cry to those who turn away in search of a better life, and yet we must sometimes turn away from those whose effect limits us—in spite of the tears.

There are those who will hate those who achieve the improved life, and yet there can be little happiness in poverty, nor love among those who must endure it.

One of the disappointments of life is that friends will abandon those who begin to change their life for the better, and yet those who remain behind will say "he has forgotten us now that he lives well." It is those who *accept* their mediocrity who choose to "remain behind." It is almost always those who have climbed *above the crowd* who would wish to return to their earlier friends and embrace them in friendship and love, knowing that they dare not, for jealousy among those who remain behind will not allow it to be so.

It is often difficult to pause in the middle of life for the purpose of sifting out the debris which we collect throughout our years. We tend to accumulate and cling to ideas that limit our progress. We cherish friendships even though the friendships impede our personal growth. We allow ourselves acquaintances, in spite of those acquaintances whose conversation affect or destroy our attitude about life and people. We maintain business associates, although those associates teach us immoral, illegal, or unethical practices. We learn shortcuts for *increasing* profits while *decreasing* quality. In countless ways, we wander through life allowing people and their attitudes and ideas to mold *our* character—people whose attitudes and ideas have brought *themselves* little in the way of progress, productivity, or happiness.

Unpopular as it may seem, each of us accumulates people, customs, attitudes, habits, opinions, and philosophies which we very simply cannot afford to keep—if we seek honestly after an improved life. Friendships are indeed valuable, but so is the human life and it is foolish to fall short of our potential because we feared alienating a good friend.

The gathering of a few business friends for lunch is a common, everyday occurrence. In one hour we can satisfy our hunger for food, gossip, ridicule, and condemnation of those not present. We can repeat half-truths brought to us through hearsay. We can complain about government, management, co-workers, traffic, taxes, weather, and the "system", while doing nothing to produce solutions. Even if the conversation *does* reveal solutions, we make no effort to communicate them to those who can possibly implement them, accepting things for the way they are.

If our attitudes, results, or happiness is to ever improve, we must exercise the painful discipline required for "weeding-out" the garden of our life. Eating alone *is* better than mingling with those whose conversation is negative. Cancelling the appointment *is* better than keeping the appointment with those who will simply waste our time. Changing the conversation *is* better than prolonging a conversation designed to degrade someone. Telling the whole, painful truth *is* better than a half-truth, distorted to make ourselves look or sound good. Saying "no" *is* better than saying "yes" to something you don't want to do, or to someone you don't want to be with. Being firm *is* better than being courteous to those whose caustic personality does not justify courtesy. The improvement of our personal circumstances means that we must learn to do what the failures are simply not willing to do.

Better than *many* of the *wrong* friends are a *few* of the *right* friends. Better than a *few* of the *wrong* friends are *no* friends at all!

Life is a delicate maneuver of selection, rejection, review and change. Each person entering our world brings either a contribution or destruction. Trying to be "always nice" is to invite certain disaster. Those with poisonous attitudes, strange opinions, and caustic conversations love to look for someone nice who will listen to them. They love to dump their verbal garbage into the mental factory of anyone willing to listen. A major challenge in life is for each person to learn the art of standing guard at the doorway of their mind. Carefully examine the credentials and authority of those seeking to enter within that place where your attitudes are formed.

The words, opinions, and comments of others are constantly taking their toll on each of us. Subtly, the conversations of gloom, despair, complaining, condemning, and criticizing are forming our temporary moods and our permanent personality and character. As a wise man once said, "A sour face does not come as an accident. It is the result of sour thoughts."

Children are often told by well-intentioned but misguided parents that they are bad, naughty, selfish, or shy. Teachers by their actions or their expressions sometimes report to the parents that their child is slow, or uncooperative, or a poor student. Throughout our early years, each of us were subjected to impulsive remarks of those who were unaware that it was those very words which were forming our character. As we become adults, we then seem to tend to choose to associate with those most like us. The weak attract the weak; the poor are most comfortable with the poor; the successful are drawn toward those who are successful; those of optimistic views and attitudes select those of *their* own kind. What we have *become* largely determines the kind of people, events, books, and lifestyle that we *select*.

If humans are ever going to change their personal and financial circumstances from one level up to another, we must accept the fact that such progress must consist of "doing" as well as "un-doing." Many of the events and people who currently influence us must be sacrificed. Those sources of doubt, worry, negativity, greed, and selfishness must be cut free, for as long as *that* influence remains, change will not likely occur. Those who attempt to change themselves or their circumstances without severing the "mental anchors" which they've attached to themselves are going to make their task nearly impossible. "Undoing" the past is difficult enough *by itself,* even *without* those who, by their conversation, remarks, or attitudes keep pulling us back toward that which we're trying to leave behind.

Imagine a man or woman who has been constantly trying to "make ends meet"—paying only a portion of their debts, buying the bargain-priced clothes, shopping to save a few pennies on a can of beans, and the countless other things which people must do when unable to earn "enough money." Finally, the day comes when the person combines the right mixture of anger, frustration, humiliation, confidence, determination, and courage to say—"Never again!" Their resolve to change themselves and their situation is unshakeable, and they thrust themselves into reading the right books, dressing the right way, thinking the right thoughts, and going to the right places. Their lives are committed toward the changing of "things" for the better.

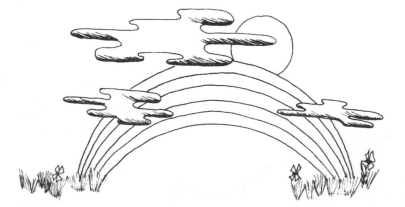

In spite of this new excitement, determination, and effort, imagine the chances for success when the man or woman must return at the end of the day to those whose voices ring with discouragement, ridicule, and exaggerated doubt. It seems as though there will always be the negative brother-in-law who is there to say—"For someone who's always been broke, you're sure putting on quite a show. Good luck!"

Being subjected to both our "new determination to succeed" as well as to those close to us whose words remind us of an unproductive past, is like being on a mental elevator ride; we move ourselves upward with our thoughts and actions, but some thoughtless person keeps pushing the "down button," bringing us back to where we mentally began. Our new confidence quickly gives way to old doubt; our new actions are overcome by old fears; and finally, we may return once more to that kind of thinking which puts people on their mental and financial knees. Having brought us back from our world of dreams, ambition, and accomplishments with their well-meant but destructive opinions, our friends celebrate by inviting us to their Friday night party where once again we will become active participants in the jokes, sarcasm, and gossip of those content with their own mediocrity. Having exchanged our dreams of a new life for the acceptance of old things, we make the quiet transition to never again try, plan, dream, explore, or achieve.

The value of surrounding yourself with the *right* friends is immeasureably awesome. The danger of surrounding yourself with the *wrong* friends can be devastating. Perhaps a good theme might be— "Friendship in proportion to the right personal growth from that friendship."

And finally, be aware that the "right" friends should not be equated to those with the "most" money. It is the attitudes, awareness, and other positive human virtues of the friends we select that are of importance. Not all poor *people* make poor *friends,* nor do all rich friends have an enriching effect on our lives. Carefully examine the "friends" you have. . . *not* their assets or accomplishments. By examining our friends from *both* ends of the financial spectrum, we may discover several of the rich as well as poor "friends" with whom we can no longer afford to associate.

III. THE VALUE OF ATTITUDES

Regardless of one's religious or intellectual inclinations, it is difficult to disbelieve that humans somehow fit into a grand scheme governed over by a power which few if any of us understand. I am personally convinced that man came from someplace. . . that his intelligence existed elsewhere before coming to this earth. I believe that his *individual* intelligence, his very existence, dwelt elsewhere, growing, learning, trying, failing, and succeeding—but *always growing.* Our three score and ten on *this* earthly sphere is but a mere stepping stone in some methodical plan of eternal progression, whereupon we shall somehow advance ourselves in a life to follow, or recede, and watch those we love—who *advanced,* rather than recede—move past us toward a new awareness, and a deeper understanding of things. Perhaps this is what "hell" and "damnation" might be. Imagine the personal agony upon discovering that we were actually being "tested," as it were, without our being aware of it, and in exchange for lasting personal growth, a deeper awareness, a new understanding, we instead elected to choose promiscuity, idleness, fault-finding, and hang-overs. And for those we most dearly loved on this earth who elected the more lasting benefits from this "earthly proving ground," their advancement occurs before our very eyes and we are left behind, helpless to do anything now to keep pace. Our eternal damnation is the awareness of the value of love, and honesty, and those other positive human virtues, and that our loved ones who possess them must now be always one step ahead in their eternal progress. Yet we can no longer speak, touch, kiss, express emotion . . . but must always be aware of their existence, although they are not aware of ours.

As I read and ponder and speculate upon people, their deeds and their destiny, I become more deeply convinced that it is our natural destiny to grow, to succeed, to prosper, and to find happiness while we're here. In a nation where opportunity abounds, it is within the reach of any human to find within his own life a personal realization of the very best of all that exists, including personal wealth. Contrary to the teaching of some religions, wealth is not evil— *poverty* is evil. For poverty (except in extreme exceptions) represses individuals, or groups of individuals who elected not to use their individual talents. They chose, rather, to allow those who *have* discovered and used *their* talents, to take care of them.

I am aware that it is said of those with divine authority that "the meek shall inherit the earth," but where does it also say that in order to be "meek" you must also be poor. That is total folly. . .that is a gross form of rationalization used by the lazy and bastardly to justify their voluntary lack of human progress. And by lazy and bastardly I clearly include those who give up in the face of difficulty—even *severe* difficulty; those who make less than a total commitment to any cause, calling, or occupation— and I most definitely include those who never even *try* to advance their situation in life through effort. Imagine Washington deciding not to try because it

looked bad across the Delaware. Imagine Lincoln *giving up* because he was embarrassed as a soldier, failed as a businessman, or was soundly defeated at the polls by his peers. Imagine John Kennedy deciding *not* to go to the moon—to make America first, both in our own eyes as well as in the eyes of the rest of the world. And imagine, if you will, a *world* without the contributions of these, and other great men who overcame adversity with talent, desire, and total determination to leave behind a world slightly better than they found it.

In the event that I have failed to make my point, let it be known here and now that God, or whatever power is behind our existence, did not intend for us to fail, or wallow in poverty, self-pity, self-martyrdom, or mediocrity in any form. Such is not the grand design for man. He is blessed with all those raw materials necessary for progress, such as imagination, ideas, inspiration, and undeveloped intellectual capacity. . . and that capacity is totally without limitation. The *only limitation* placed on our abilities is our *inability* to easily recognize our unlimited nature. It takes effort to become aware of our staggering and limitless abilities. It takes effort to

become enthusiastic over a cause, or an occupation. It takes effort to continue when our results—as well as our friends—tell us to give up trying. It takes effort to feel right about everything that happens—the joy as well as the sorrows of life. And it also takes effort to learn to love ourselves above all others, especially when we are so consciously aware of our failures, doubts and tragedies. It does not, however, take effort to fail. It requires little else than a slowly deteriorating attitude about our present, our future, and about ourselves. It is ironic that one of the few things in this life over which we have total control is our own attitudes, and yet most of us live our entire life behaving as though we had no control whatsoever. By our attitude, we decide to read, or not to read. By our attitude, we decide to try or give up. By our attitude, we blame ourselves for our failure, or we foolishly blame others. Our attitude determines whether we love or hate, tell the truth or lie, act or procrastinate, advance or recede, and by our own attitude we and we alone actually decide whether to succeed or fail.

How incredibly unique that a God who would create the complex and immense universe would create the human race and give to those humans the free choice that would permit them to select their own achievement or their own destruction.

This strange but all-knowing God gave to us a delicately balanced sphere called earth, and on it, he placed the intelligent human who would either develop it or destroy it. How terribly fascinating that God would leave both projects—earth as well as humans—unfinished! Across the rivers and streams he built no bridges; he left the pictures unpainted, the song unsung, the book unwritten, and space unexplored. For the accomplishment of those things, God created the unfinished human, who—within his heart and mind, had the capacity to do all these things and more, depending upon his own choice. Attitude determines choice, and choice determines results. All that we are, and all that we can become has indeed been left unto us.

At this very moment in time, as you read these words, your attitude has determined what you are. Your enthusiams, intensity, faith in yourself, patience with yourself and others, and childish excitement about your boundless future is a result of that single word—attitude. The work of God is finished, but the work of creating your better future has just begun. For as long as you continue to draw breath, you have the chance to finish that work, and in so doing, complete the work in and for the earth and for yourself that God has left undone. In the cycles and seasons of life, attitude is everything!

IV. THE CONSTANT, PREDICTABLE PATTERN OF CHANGE

The tide comes in and then recedes; the sun rises, giving light, and then sets, bringing darkness. Drought plagues the farm fields of the world, followed by rain in abundance. On this day, we swelter under the intense heat of the August sun, and soon we clothe ourselves against the penetrating cold of the mid-winter storm. Prosperity brings her abundant opportunity and rewards, but will withdraw at a future time when confronted by a receding business climate. The smile gives way to the tear, as does the joy to the sorrow and the jubilation to the tragedy. Close friends become hated enemies. The guns and bloodshed of war are followed by the stillness of a temporary peace.

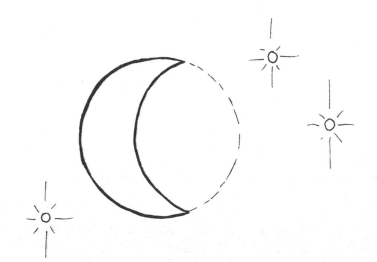

For each of us existing on this spinning blue-white sphere called earth, confidence is replaced, with the passage of time, by doubt; patience is replaced by stress; expectancy by boredom; and achievement by disillusionment.

As the wheel of life continues its constant turn, all human emotions appear, disappear, and appear once again. We sit in amazement in the role of spectators, as a generation living in morality becomes an immoral generation, giving us cause to predict the end of the world, as did our forefathers when confronted by the same dilemma generations before.

The confrontations, disappointments, and challenges of life are treated by each generation as though they are the first to experience such events, when in fact, the pre-Christian years saw the same occurrences both appear and dissolve.

For all of us, the only constant factor in life is our feelings and attitudes toward life. A major challenge faced by us all is that we learn to experience the changing *of* life's cycles without being changed *by* them. To make a constant and conscious effort to improve *ourselves* in face of changing *circumstances* is to assure a tolerance for the winters of life's events, and to permit ourselves the full *enjoyment* of the blessings of life's harvest come the autumn.

Springtime
the time to take advantage of
opportunity
friendship
love
ideas

Nora

V. THE SPRING

Following the turbulence of winter comes the season of activity and opportunity called springtime. It is the season for entering the fertile fields of life with seed, knowledge, commitment, and a determined effort. It is not a time to linger, nor to ponder the possibility of failure. Foolish is the one who would allow springtime to pass while dwelling upon the memory of the successful crop of last fall, or the *failure* to reap last fall in spite of the massive efforts of last spring.

It is a natural characteristic of springtime to present itself ever so briefly, or to lull us into inactivity with its bounteous beauty. Do not pause too long to soak in the aroma of the blossoming flowers, lest you awaken to find springtime gone with your seed still in your sack. Spring does not care if you sow or sleep, nor does it care if you plant abundantly or meagerly. It does not care if you plant the fertile kernel of wheat or useless weed-seeds. Neither spring, nor the soil, sun, or other elements care if you plant at all. It will merely present itself as the time to take advantage. Springtime will not admonish you to plant, nor will it warn of the consequences of *not* planting. For the tiller of the soil, springtime is without emotion. It was *God* who gave *you* the wisdom to rise from your comfortable chair and enter the fields at the right season.

For the husband, father, wife, mother, or businessperson, springtime comes in the form of opportunity to enroll in a class, or to have a conversation with someone at the proper moment—to have the courage to change either occupation or residence—or perhaps even to change your mind about something or someone. The springtime of life manifests itself infrequently. Do not allow springtime to pass while you sit idly, contemplating the severity of the past winter of life.

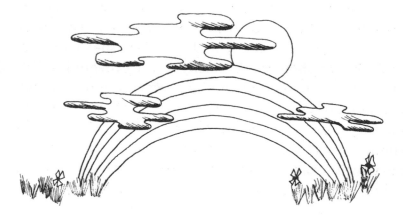

With the intelligence, wisdom, and freedom of choice given to us as humans, exercise the discipline to plant *in spite of* the rocks, weeds, or other obstacles before us. The rocks, weeds, and thorns of the world cannot destroy all your seeds if you plant massively enough and intelligently enough.

To take full advantage of the spring, rid your soil of the weeds and rocks disguised as the opinions of those around you in the form of worry, doubt, or pessimism. It is the fertilizer of faith and enthusiasm that will overcome the worst forms of bugs and weeds. Listen not to the bearers of discouraging words—those who would have you rest with them during the work season of spring. They will find themselves starving come the fall and winter, or begging from those who recognize spring as a brief opportunity to work, and to leave play for another season.

The essence of springtime is faith woven among the threads of massive human effort. Springtime is the fresh air of new opportunity, amid the dissipating clouds of winter. Spring is the time for entering the bleak, empty fields given to us as a new chance. When we enter those fields, we see in the adjoining fields the blossoming of *nature's* flowers—the daisies, and other miracles of nature which God planted, reminding us now that nature fulfills *its* promises. Already, the miracle of the seasons shows itself, for the same snows that gave us cause to huddle for warmth during the winter also covered nature's crops which exist now before our eyes. Expend *your* effort now, without complaint, without doubt, without pessimism, and without self-pity over the severity of your winter of circumstance. Did the daisies complain because of the same cold and the same winds? No, they did not, yet they exist as either a reminder, or a threat, or a promise. Do the lilies hide beneath the cover of earth, fearing an unexpected return of winter, or do they restrain themselves for fear of the coming bugs and weeds of summer? Do the daisies or the lilies of the field of nature make excuses, or lie, or linger? They are there because they endured circumstance, and pushed aside the seasonal obstacles of rocks and hard-packed soil, and so must you if *your* life is to blossom. The same God who gave life and meaning and opportunity to the crops of nature now gives to you the same blessings. Are you to say that you are less than a lily, or a daisy? Do they have a brain or vision or choice? Do they converse one with another for the sharing of ideas?

Springtime merely says—"Here I am!" Springtime sends its life, and its warmth. It sends us constant messages of its arrival—the robin, the squirrels, the return of the swallows, and the berries of the field for those whose own storehouses are empty. Springtime gives a smile to those who respond to its arrival, and a tear for those who sit, or who make only half an effort. Some will work only a little—enough to give to themselves excuses for the meager results come the fall. Some will fish, or play, or sleep, or lie among the wildflowers. Some will plant foolishly, or quickly, not taking the time to perform to the level of their capability or intelligence. Some will trust only in the God who brought forth the wildflowers, forgetting the admonition that "faith without works is dead." The warmth, the sun,

and the fertile fields of the spring are but part of the
formula for achievement; the catalyst that produces
the final result is intense, honest, and consistent
human effort, and therein lies the problem. As
humans, we are given free agency—the right to
choose, the right to use discipline, or not use it. The
choice to act with courage, or huddle in fear. The
choice to think, or respond out of habit. When we are
given free choice, more often than not, we choose
rest, or we choose half an effort, or we choose a
convenient excuse. Sometimes we choose to remain
indoors because of its comfort, or by a brook rather
than in the field, knowing that the intelligence that
lets us perform well will also let us lie well, or excuse
ourselves well, or blame circumstances well. Above
all, the gift of human intelligence and the freedom of
choice that accompanies it is not a blessing, but a
curse, for it allows us to even fool, and lie to
ourselves, which is the height of ignorance.

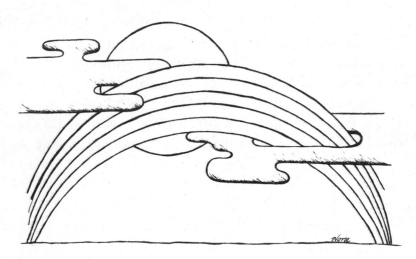

Choose action, not rest. Choose truth, not fantasy. Choose a smile, not a frown. Choose love, not animosity. Choose the good in life in all things, and choose the opportunity as well as the chance to work when springtime smiles on your life.

Much of the effort and opportunity of springtime rests in the depth and degree of our faith. Life provides no assurances that the planting of seeds will provide the reaping of crops. We have only the demonstrated experiences of others to draw upon. The weather storms of life *could* cancel our efforts expended in the fields of opportunity. But to expend *no* effort during the spring will *assure no results* during the fall.

Faith further provides to us an irrevocable law decreed in heaven which assures that for every disciplined human effort we will receive a multiple reward. . .for each cup planted, a bushel reaped. . . for every good idea given to another, many shall be given to us in return. . .for every demonstrated act of faith, a multiplicy of the rewards. . .for every act of love given, a life of love in return. . .for each seed of encouragement given to another, a gathering of the strength of our own courage. . .for each hour of honest effort expended during the spring, an hour of *honest* rest in the fall. . .for each act of patience and understanding rendered to another, a return of patience from another when our own acts give cause for disappointment.

It is the promise of spring that as we sow, so shall we also reap. Sow lies, reap lies; sow greed, reap poverty; sow inactivity, reap an empty storehouse; choose to procrastinate, and surely an infant giant will grow to become a monster rendering your future action ineffective.

The act of planting during the warm breezes of spring requires that we exert the pain of human discipline, and being unwilling to do so assures that in the coming fall, we shall surely experience the greater pain of regret—the difference is that the pain of discipline weighs ounces, and the pain of regret weighs tons. We *must* either plant during the springtime of life, or beg from others during the fall.

A kernel of corn produces its own kind: A seed of doubt, or fear, or distrust placed in the mind also produces after its own kind. As certainly as the soil gives back like unto that which we place into it, so also does the mind of man give back in human circumstance that which we place into it by our choice of human thought. The price, or effort of thinking thoughts of love, prosperity, or self-confidence is no greater than the price given to thoughts of hate, poverty, or self-doubt. Only the rewards are different.

Each day is given to us as a new season of spring. The thoughts, deeds, dreams, and efforts of today will provide tomorrow's harvest. To neglect the opportunity given to us *this* day is to delay our better *future*. Do not use today to mentally re-live yesterday or to await the arrival of tomorrow, for tomorrow— when it arrives—will be called *today*. There will be no better day, no better opportunity, no better springtime, no better time to begin than the current moment. Seize the moments as you find them and mold them into your own better future. Today's procrastination will surely be tomorrow's regret.

For some, the emergence of springtime is a time of great difficulty. Perhaps because of our own neglect or inactivity of past seasons, we find our storehouse and our stomachs empty. Our need for food or monies is not in the coming fall. . .but now. The voices of those we love echo their needs brought about by our lack of effort or results, and their eyes look away from us, lest we detect the shame and disappointment shown in them.

Under circumstances such as these we are often given to forget that the seasons will neither speed up nor slow down because of our needs. The springtime will only *appear*, but it will not wait, nor will it transform seed into harvest. As always, the seed as well as our needs must await the changing seasons. We cannot ask nature for an advance. Talent, need, desire, and prayer are meaningless to those suffering the painful consequences of earlier neglect—and with empty stomachs, barren storehouse, and great regret we must enter the fields during *this* spring, for to neglect once again because of our demeaning circumstances is to assure a continuance of the current conditions.

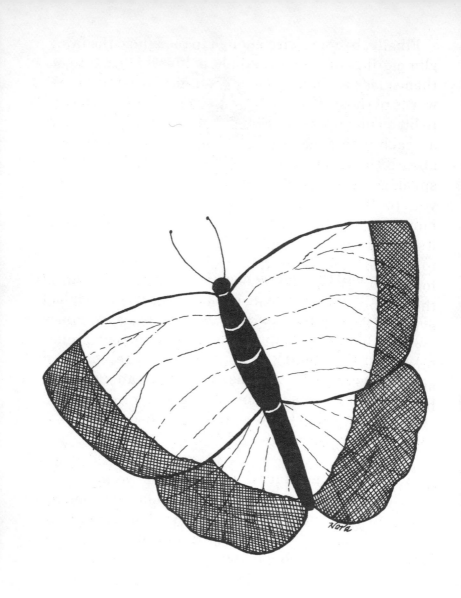

Finally, become wise enough to recognize the faint glimmerings of the springtimes of life which manifest themselves each day; the opportunity to listen to the words of those wiser than ourselves; the opportunity to lift a child upon your knee; the opportunity to walk a beach with someone you love; the opportunity to absorb the value of a good book; the opportunity to speak good things of someone, when habit prompts you to find fault; the opportunity to watch the hummingbirds, or the flowers, or a butterfly perform its strange miracle; seize the infrequent opportunity to do *nothing* for a change, or *something* for a change; force yourself to turn off the television, and embrace the opportunity for having family conversation—or even silence. Opportunity surrounds us all, appearing and disappearing just as fast, leaving behind fond memories to those who responded to its appearance, or regret to those who were then too busy to bother.

Life is truly a constant beginning, a constant opportunity, a constant springtime. We need only to learn to look once again at life as we did as children, letting fascination and curiosity give us welcome cause for taking a second look, rather than taking for granted. Fortune, happiness, and peace of mind await those who learn to look for the miraculous hidden among the common. The unique blending of sun, soil, and seed at the springtime of seasons will provide predictable and miraculous results for those who will learn to take full and complete advantage of the spring.

Summertime
...a time to protect and nurture

Success in life is not an easy matter, nor is it an easy matter for the seed to push away the soil in its quest to find the light and the airborne chemicals that give it health. Progress in any form and happiness or success in any form requires constant effort, for obstacles exist that might discourage the weak and the undeserving. Overcome one obstacle in life, and another appears to fill the void. Life is designed to be a story of achievement *in spite of* adversity, not in the absence of adversity, for without adversity achievement could not exist. Do not blame the problems and challenges of life for your humbling circumstances. Does the seed complain because of the rocks it must grow over, under, around, or through? Would any worthy life exist on earth, if all life were to surrender when first confronted by difficulty? The constant, unrelenting pull of life is downward—giving cause for disappointment, despair, and discouragement. There shall always be cause to give up; there shall always be cause for complaint, but engage in complaining and you add to the downward pull of life. The only automatic thing in life is weeds and bugs. They need not be planted, nor cared for. Their existence is assumed in that they feed and survive on the good efforts of the industrious.

The summer of life is a time to protect; it is a time for constant daily effort to guard against the busy bugs and the noxious weeds. The spring is a time for the *creation* of things of value, and those things require the season of summer for *growing* and gaining strength that they might yield their result in the coming fall. The end of spring cannot bring an end of human effort—one effort ends and another remains yet to begin. When effort ceases, when neglect makes it haunting appearance, growth gives way to stagnation and decay. The bugs and weeds of life exist to test the human will to succeed, and the human worthiness for life's rich rewards.

Develop an understanding and awareness of the fact that all good will be attacked. It is nature's way of qualifying those who are worthy and those who are not. The weeds of life are designed to turn confidence into doubt, trust into suspicion, patience into impatience, and effort into procrastination, worry, and eventual defeat. Do not spend valuable time arguing with nature. The weeds, bugs, rocks, and storms of life will all laugh at those who take time to viciously accuse them of being unfair. Unfair, yes, but often to those who seek something for nothing, or who seek the rewards of life without paying the price of waging war against obstacles by increased activity and determination. Spend no time chasing the birds who seek to peck at your seeds, or the bugs who seek to devour your coming harvest. For those who make diligent efforts to plant, protect, and preserve there are not enough birds, bugs, or other obstacles to destroy *all* the efforts of last spring.

Learn to accept the perpetual existence of negativity, and learn also that negativity always yields to constant human effort coupled with the constantly growing human faith and attitude. It is written that as you sow, so also shall you reap, but only when you combine the efforts of sowing with the mental effort of believing, and the physical effort of constant attention to those things of value. Smile at adversity, and act quickly to eliminate it. Expect adversity, for it shall surely appear. Be grateful for adversity, for it forces the human spirit to grow—for surely, the human character is formed not in the *absence* of difficulty but in our *response* to difficulty.

All things, even adversity, have their worthy
purpose.

Both of us—I, the writer of this book, and you, the reader of this book—live in a world of causes and consequences. The harvest, which is our life as we now live it, is the result of seeds planted at an earlier time. Some of the "seeds" we planted ourselves, through unbreakable habits. Others were planted *for* us by parents, teachers, and other well-meaning, but often misguided people whose own poor thinking habits were passed on to us. In either case, our current attitude, finances, environment, lifestyle, and our view of our own future possibilities are called circumstances—and to change circumstances, we must change the *cause* of those circumstances, which is ourselves. We must change our habits, our attitudes, our opinions, and often our occupation, residence, and even friends, if circumstances are ever to change.

A man visits the shop of a gardener and, without thinking or even inquiring, selects what appears to be an attractive plant which he purchases, takes home and plants in the ground in his yard. Months later he discovers that the plant has grown, matured, and now blossoms into a healthy bougainvillea, to which he is allergic. To wish now that the plant were a rose, or a tulip, would be foolish. The circumstances will not change because he dislikes the result. . .he alone is the cause of his watery eyes and running nose. And so it is with the person who lives amid mediocrity—whether the seeds which brought about that condition were placed into the soil of life by himself or by someone else is unimportant. To accuse others, to feel sorry for ourselves, or to continue rationalizing or making excuses is foolish. Only a massive, voluntary, and effective assault on changing *causes* is important. Direct your thought, conversation, and full attention to *that* if you wish to change circumstances; concentrate a good share of your idle hours upon self-development by planning more, reading more, and investing more. Invest your time in worthy projects; invest your thoughts toward a worthy purpose; invest your talents toward a worthy occupation; invest your affection toward a worthy recipient; and finally, reserve your greatest respect for yourself, for it is *that* image. . .what you preceive *yourself* to *be*. . .that determines the quality of life.

Let's face it . . . people and events are going to continue to both hurt and disappoint you. Among the people will be those you most love, as well as those you least know. Seldom is it their intent to purposely hurt you, but rather, a variety of situations mostly beyond your control will cause them to act, speak, or think in ways which can have an adverse effect upon you, your present feelings and emotions, and the way your life unfolds. It has been this way through six thousand years of recorded history, and your hurt or grief is not the first time a human has been deeply hurt by the inappropriate actions of another. The only way to avoid being touched by life—the good as well as the bad—is to withdraw from society, and even then you will disappoint yourself, and your imaginings about what is going on out there will haunt you and hurt you. Knowing this, there is but one solution that will support you when people and events hurt you—and that is to learn to work harder on your own personal growth than anything else. Since you cannot control the weather, or the traffic, or the one you love, or your neighbors, or your boss, then you must learn to control *you* . . . the one whose response to the difficulties of life really counts.

Do not doubt yourself, for where doubt resides, confidence cannot. Do not neglect yourself, for with neglect comes loss. Do not imagine yourself to be less than you are, nor more than you are, but seek always to become all of which you are capable. Do not allow yourself to become arrogant or discourteous, for both are characteristics adopted by those who seek to cover their weaknesses. Do not spend time regretting the past, but invest that time wisely by preparing a better future. You are a fertile seed of the creator of all things, destined not to lie dormant, but to spring forth from the soil called life, and grow upward toward the unlimited horizons— overcoming all obstacles in the process. It is your destiny to tap your talents and to achieve all that of which you believe yourself to be worthy. . .to love more, anticipate more, overcome more, plan more attract more, and to enjoy more than you ever dreamed possible. Such is the standard of life awaiting your mental decision and outstretched hand. You are deserving—you are becoming—and you shall succeed.

The Fall

...a time for harvesting the fruits of our springtime labor

Nora

THE FALL

I like spring, but it is too young. I like summer, but it is too proud. So I like best of all autumn, because its leaves are a little yellow, its tone mellower, its colors richer, and it is tinged a little with sorrow. . . Its golden riches speak not of the innocence of spring, nor of the power of summer, but of the mellowness and kingly wisdom of approaching age. It knows the limitations of life and is content.

— Lin Yutang

Fall is a time for exultation as well as a time for a searching of the conscience. For those who planted abundantly in the spring, and who fought against the bugs, weeds, and weather of summer, fall can bring rewards which give cause for rejoicing. For those who *watched* both the arrival and departure of spring, and who made little effort to take advantage of its almost momentary tenure, fall can be a time of turmoil, a time of anxiety, and a time of great regret.

It is in the fall when we discovered how long or short the winter will be. The fall tells us if we have *really* done that which is required, or if we have fooled ourselves through the temporary anesthetic of conversation and pretense . . . of telling ourselves we've worked when we haven't.

The soil, and the arrival of fall, together occupy the seat of judgment which presents the final truth of human effort. There can be no disputing its final verdict, for the evidence of toil, care, and patience are indisputable . . . either the crops are bounteous or they are not, and if not, we need look no further than to the hands of those who were charged with responsiblity last spring. The excuses of poor soil, poor seed, or bad weather are better left unsaid, for the sower selected the soil; the sower selected the seed; the sower alone is held accountable for his crops—not circumstance.

Nothing is more exciting than a bounteous crop, and nothing more dreadful than a barren field in the fall.

So it is with those given the responsibility for planting the crops of the field, and so it is also to those who are given the responsibilities of life and success in the world of business and labor. An unproductive and meager result in the season reserved for harvesting makes confession of our own past failures both difficult and necessary.

An empty bank account is a sign of an ineffective past effort. It is a sign of a missed opportunity. It is a sign of too much procrastination, or laziness. The law of the universe is faultless. It applies equally well to the farmer as to the business person. The law is equally applied to all things and all people. The law has endured since the creation of the world, and for that long, men have sought to circumvent it, or argue with it, and even to ignore it. In the end, our results demonstrate if we have obeyed its orders, or disobeyed. The law is simple, and known to all. The law is

"As you sow, so shall you reap."

In all areas of the human existence, be aware that what we put into this world, we get back from it. It is nature's way of "evening the score." Both thoughts and actions determine the result, the lifestyle, and the human attitude. Lies, sooner or later, attract lies in return. Finding an easier way at the expense of quality will take its inevitable toll in decreased profits and sleepless nights. All effort, be it service, marketing, recruiting, or products must bring good to all those who are involved or the effort will not withstand the final test of time.

Corn planted in the spring will produce corn in the fall, as will wheat, barley, or melons produce after *their* own kind. You cannot plant one crop and expect to reap another just because you change your mind during mid-summer.

It is a tendency of humans to look about those who enjoy success as having been, at some earlier time, either lucky or dishonest. Surely, the man driving the luxury car toward his expensive home on the hill could not deserve it through hard work and sacrifice. Such is the language of the poor. For the fortunate man with the car and the house on the hill, these are crops given to him in his fall of the business season—as *just rewards* for efforts expended during an earlier springtime of his life . . . a springtime during which those who now condemn the man possibly sat back and laughed, or fished, or told stories. This is the folly of man. Those who do not possess will always scorn the possessor.

Those who condemn the successful man or woman for their apparent good fortune or dishonesty are unaware of the price often paid for success. They cannot see the massive disappointments, the shattered hopes, or the broken dreams. They do not understand the risks incurred in both raising and investing capital for an idea yet unproven. They do not see the legal involvements, the tax burdens, the challenges of labor, or the restraining governmental regulations, nor do they appreciate the family dissent that seems to automatically accompany the pursuit of success. Those who condemn see and scorn the result, being unaware of the cost as well as cause which produced the success. For so long as the selfish of the world scorn the successful, that long will they continue to live as they live.

In the fall, we either enjoy, or we excuse. For those who failed to take full advantage of the spring, who failed to guard their crops carefully throughout the heat of summer, there can be no legitimate reasons . . . only excuses, and excuses are merely apologetic attempts to place blame on circumstances rather than on ourselves.

The difference between an inadequate apartment and a mansion on the hill is the same as the difference between *average* effort in the spring, and *massive* effort in the spring. Nature always promises that a cup produces a bushel . . . that we will receive *more* than we plant. Knowing this, as all of us do, we forget that to reap *many* bushels, which is the measure of success, we still must plant *many* cups. Massive action in the spring of life still is the requirement for massive success in the fall. Forty hours a week spent in the fields of opportunity may not be enough, especially if it is spent in the wrong field. Sometimes, to improve our results we must make the painful admission that our present field is too rocky, or thorny, or that the fertile soil is too shallow. And while there is great difficulty involved in changing one field for another more fertile field, *that* difficulty is insignificant compared to the *ultimate difficulty that comes from not changing.*

The Season of Winter...

THE WINTER

Winter, like spring, is a season which can make its brief appearance during *any* season, as a brief reminder of its ultimate power. In mid-summer while we consciously tend our carefully planted crops, winter can momentarily descend upon us as if threatening to take away the fruits of our efforts. Winter can make its threatening appearance during the season of opportunity—the spring—and if we do not quickly respond to cancel its potentially devastating effect, the season of opportunity will be taken from us by one of the storms of life, leaving us with yet another full year of waiting. Winter can prematurely appear during the season of harvest—the fall—just as we are about to reap the rewards of expended human effort, and leave us with crops—or results—which are of little value.

The first great lesson of life to learn is that winter will always come. Not only the winter of cold, and wind, and ice, and snow, but the human winters of despair and loneliness, or disappointment, or tragedy. It is winter when prayers go unanswered, or when the acts of our children leave us shaken and stunned. It is winter when the economy turns against us, or when creditors come after us. It is winter when competition threatens, or when a friend takes advantage. Winter comes in many forms, and at any time, both to the planter of crops as well as to the person in business, or even to our personal lives.

The arrival of winter finds us in one of two categories: Either we are *prepared* or we are *unprepared*.

To those who are prepared, who have planted abundantly in the spring, guarded their crops carefully during the summer, and harvested massively during the fall, winter can be yet another season of *opportunity.* It can be a time for reading, a time for planning, a time for gathering our strength for the coming spring, and a time for taking comfortable shelter. It can be a time of great enjoyment, a time to be shared with those we love, and with those with whom we have labored. It is a time of thanksgiving, and a time for the sharing of life's bounteous gifts. Winter is a time for being grateful, both for what we have, as well as for what we can yet achieve. Winter is a time for rest, but not *excessive* rest. It is a time to enjoy the fruits of our labors, but not a time for gluttony. It is a time for warm conversations, but not a time for gossip. It is a time of gratitude, but not a time for complacency. It is a time to be proud, but not a time to be egotistical.

What we do with our time, with ourselves, with our friends, and with our attitudes during the season of winter determines what we will do with the coming spring. We are meant to constantly *improve* our conditions, ourselves, and our results. We either improve, or we regress, for never do we remain the same. If we do not improve, it is because we do not use our intelligence, our reasoning, and our full potential—and finally, what we do *not* use, we lose. Through lack of use we may lose our intelligence, reasoning, potential, and strength. And when lack of use, or misuse, costs us these worthy human attributes, we predictably *regress.*

Again, it is a basic law of life that demands either human progression or human regression.

To those who are *prepared* for winter's arrival, let them use winter as they would use spring . . . to take advantage.

To those who are unprepared, the arrival of winter is a time for regret and a time for sorrow. Having lacked the willingness to pay the pain of earlier discipline, we now pay the heavier pain of regret. The burdens and chains of discipline would seem insignificant when compared to the massive weights and cumbersome restraints of regret. Regret is an empty storehouse and an empty kitchen when the coming fall is yet a full year away. Even with the arrival of spring, our efforts will be expended with an empty stomach and an empty purse. To the prepared, winter is springtime in yet another form, but to those who are ill-prepared, winter's arrival is full of horror and uncertainty. Love and harmony give way to accusations and anger.

The time to experience the horror of a winter for which we are unprepared is in the springtime, and in our mind. Let the imagination paint for us the chilling winds, snow-blown fields, and ice covered trees; let us experience in our mind's eye the wailing of a hungry child, and the disappointment showing in the eyes of the one we love; let us emotionally experience the fumbling for excuses, and apologies for our past mistakes, and the fear that comes with a knock on the door, or the delivery of the mail. Anticipating these scenes in advance can provide the shock that moves us into massive effort in the spring, that those efforts might prevent our horrified imaginings from becoming reality.

Throughout all the seasons of the year, winter can touch our lives in many small ways . . . testing us, and providing us with subtle reminders of the plight of those whose lives are surrounded by winter. Winter can be a lost opportunity, or the loss of love. A winter is when a trusted friend gives you cause for disappointment, or when expected business goes to a competitor. A frigid blast from the cold, harsh words of someone you love is winter, and so is the pessimism or cynicism from someone whose advice and counsel you seek.

The major challenge confronting those surrounded by winter is to not let it affect the arrival of spring, and our ability to *recognize* that arrival. Much of life is in learning to always remain part of the solution rather than allowing ourselves to become part of the problem.

If you are without love, money, or employment, it is a winter, and its very appearance is because you've missed a springtime somewhere. Neglect is always costly, and winter is merely a circumstance—an *effect* brought on by some *earlier cause*. Dwelling upon the severity of your personal winter merely makes the winter more difficult to endure. Search the inner confines of your mind and your soul for the purpose of discovering the real cause within *you*. Adversity is seldom attributable to some *one,* or some *thing* outside of ourselves. To blame outside influences for the circumstance of winter is a convenient excuse for misplacing responsibility. It is the normal human tendency to place blame for a winter of life on someone else, which is why most humans reap the *result* of mediocrity that accompanies such behavior.

For things or circumstances to change, human attitudes, opinions, and habits must change. Conversation on how *things* ought to be . . . on why *things* aren't fair . . . is just that—conversation! Unproductive conversation is what the lazy and unambitious engage in during the winters of life, for there is a certain euphoria that such empty conversation produces which dulls the senses from the harsh reality of how "things" *really* are. The same euphoria is found in television and those who use it as an escape from their own empty life. It is found in alcohol and other drugs used by those seeking solutions in external means. It is found through idle gossip which allows those who engage in it to overlook their on weaknesses by attacking the weaknesses of others.

Let winter find you planning for the arrival of spring, not contemplating the errors of commission and ommission of last year. Let winter find you with a joyful countenance and a happy heart . . . with a good word for all those around you; with confidence in the future, not apprehension; with appreciation of the past, not regret; and finally, with gratitude for your achievements, adversities, and uncertainties of life, for each is a form of blessing which removes all limitations from the future possibilities of life.

Winter is a time for examining, pondering, and introspection. It is a time for re-evaluating both purpose and procedure—for rediscovering an often misplaced sense of purpose. It is a time for finding new ways for solving old dilemmas, and for devising unique plans for contributing to others, less fortunate than ourselves. It is a time for understanding and controlling anger, that frequent human emotion which causes us to pass judgment without fair deliberation. It is a time to analyze our fairness and to overcome our tendency to hastily spew forth *condemnation* without full *investigation,* for such is the height of ignorance. Winter is a time for being sincere with ourselves, about ourselves, when the tendency is to fool ourselves. It is a time for developing the skills that allow us to get along with *imperfect* people, for even a fool can get along with *perfect* people. It is also a time for becoming wise enough to know what to say—as well as to know what to *overlook* and what *not* to say. The wisdom that comes with the careful use of winter teaches us also that evolution is merely revolution at a slower pace, and that constant gradual change is the order of the universe. Only those worthy human attributes of honesty, loyalty, love, and trust in God and in our fellow man are meant to remain constant. Winter is a time for being grateful for our achievements, or for having endured our *lack* of achievement.

The physically inactive season of winter is a time for adding to our storehouse of knowledge through continued education, which in truth, does not mean learning things that we do not know, but in learning to behave as we do not now behave. The facts and things of life are automatically learned by each of us when we become inspired with the excitement of high expectation and belief in our own abilities.

With winter comes the opportunity to catch up on unkept promises, and on unanswered letters. It is a time also for encouraging the young, who with their inexperience are insecure . . . and for encouraging the old, who *because* of their experience, are apprehensive of the future. Let not winter go by without investing much of your time in assuring, teaching and encouraging others. For in so doing, your reward will be an uplifted confidence in yourself; the teacher is always the greatest recipient of the lessons he seeks to teach to others. Let winter find you thinking first of someone else, and appreciating, and being kind, and being gentle . . . and by all means, let winter find you laughing more, even though the winds blow cold, and the snows cover the soil which will soon bring new life.

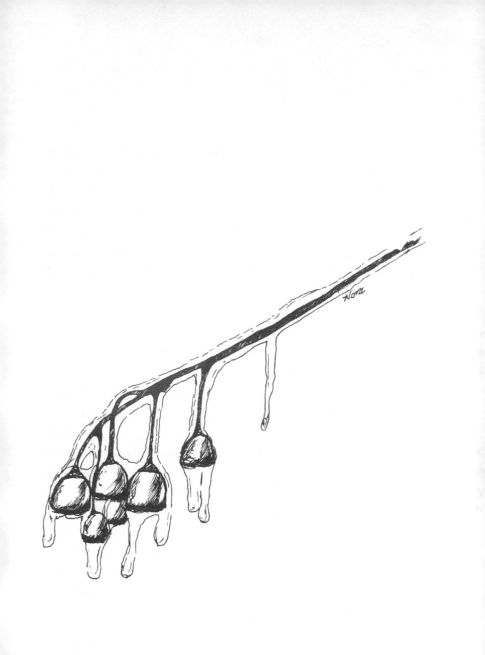

DEFEAT — THE BEST BEGINNING

Someone once said—"Don't pray for things to be easier, rather, pray for more *obstacles* and more *challenges*, for it is out of *these* that man's *character* and will to succeed are formed." Nearly every success story that I am aware of began when the person first lay flat on his mental and financial back. In this condition, people usually become sufficiently disgusted to reach deep down inside and pull out talents, abilities, desire, and determination—the basic essentials required of anyone wishing for things to get better. It is in the face of adversity that things begin to change, and the "things" always change as a result of the personal change that takes place. I have discovered that "things" never change—not by themselves. It's when a human, with sufficient disgust, desire, and determination to change his life finally steps up to the bar of human justice and shouts for all the world to hear—"I have had it with defeat and humiliation, and I will tolerate it no longer." That is when time, fate and circumstances call a hasty conference, and all three wearily agree—"We had best step aside, because we are powerless to stop that kind of resolve." But the masses of people unfortunately *don't* change—they wait for circumstances to change—blaming others, or blaming situations for their meager process. They accept defeat as though it were nature's design for humanity to wallow in pools of defeat and self-pity.

But . . . life is going to continue . . . even though you may now be defeated. The world will wake up tomorrow just as it did today, and events will continue to unfold with repeated regularity. Your role of present failure, or success, is a *temporary* condition. You will *rebound from* failure as surely as you *gravitated into* failure. The condition of any person who feels defeated and ashamed is being repeated by thousands of humans somewhere in this country at this same moment in time. Someone once suggested to me that I should say to myself, "This too shall pass" each time I was tempted to think I had accepted all the negativity and failure that my life could tolerate. Of all those who at this moment are mentally, spiritually, and financially exhausted, a few will grasp for a new beginning and, on finding it, will pull themselves to their feet and move back into the world to not only *do well*, but leave their mark indelibly impressed upon the business, political, or social world. They will be written about, talked about, and examined by their peers in numerous ways. The world will then pass judgment upon them as being "lucky" in some way, and will be unaware of the agony and loneliness which each one experienced *before* they began their march upward toward accomplishment. So, foolish as it may sound, thank God for your present limitations or failure, if that should be the case, for you now occupy a status from which nearly all success stories originate. You can go where you want to go, do what you want to do, become what you want to become . . . right from where you are. Longfellow began there—so did

Michaelangelo and Lincoln. Rod Serling wrote 40 stories before one was accepted. Disney was dismissed by a newspaper which felt he had no talent. Richard Byrd crashed his plane the first two times he soloed and went on to become one of the world's great explorers. So be grateful for your adversity. But for your own better future, may it work *for* you, not *against* you. The world will willingly stand by and let you feel sorry for yourself—until you finally die broke and alone—if that's what you want. It will also *stand aside* for you once you firmly decide that your present situation is only temporary, and that you will get back up and go on to make your mark. The world doesn't really have time to care which choice you make, so for yourself at least, give a run at adventure, with your eyes firmly set on achievement, not merely existence and self-pity.

From this moment on, and for what remains of the balance of your life, make your commitment to excellence, remembering that it is your challenge to succeed. After all, you only have one life! Lets do something remarkable!

Do not walk in front of me,
I may not follow.

Do not walk behind me,
I may not lead.

But walk beside me,
And be my friend.

E. James Rohn
Founder, Chairman
of the Board
Jim Rohn Productions

Direct all inquiries
regarding this book, or other
products and services of
Mr. E. James Rohn
To
Jim Rohn Productions
2091 Business Center Drive
Irvine, California 92715
(714) 851-8244